How to
Design
Beautiful
Cakes

Elaine A. Daveson

CHILD & ASSOCIATES
AN ALL-AUSTRALIAN PUBLISHER

Acknowledgements

I would like to thank Mrs Pat Rudorfer for her assistance in
the preparation of the cakes.

Published by Child & Associates Publishing Pty Ltd,
5 Skyline Place, Frenchs Forest, NSW, Australia, 2086
Co-published outside Australia and New Zealand by
Merehurst Press
5 Great James Street, London WC1N 3DA, England
This book has been edited and designed in Australia by
the Publisher
First edition 1989
Text by Elaine Daveson
Photography by Mike Hallson
© Elaine Daveson 1989
Edited by Carol Jacobson
Printed in Singapore by Toppan Printing Co. (S) Pte Ltd
Typesetting processed by Deblaere Typesetting Pty Ltd

National Library of Australia
Cataloguing-in-Publication

Daveson, Elaine.
   How to design beautiful cakes.

   Includes index.
   ISBN 0 86777 165 8.

   1. Cake decorating. I. Title.

641.8'653

Back cover: *A tapering floral spray showing graduated flower sizes surrounded by leaves and ribbon
loops.*

Half title: *A beautifully balanced three-tiered wedding cake with floral sprays and scalloped extension
work on each tier. The top spray winds up and around a tiny violin.*

Title: *An offset four-tiered wedding cake with ribbon strips edged with lace used to direct attention to the
floral sprays on each tier. The spray on the large tier has been extended upwards to balance the weight of
the cakes.*

Contents

Introduction 8

Principles of Design 10
Unity 12
Harmony and Contrast 13
Balance 19
Repetition, Rhythm and Progression 25
Proportion 27
Emphasis 29

Elements of Design 33
Shape 34
Line 34
Space 41
Texture 46
Colour 48

Masterpiece of Design 59
Impact 61

Index 63

Introduction

While there are many books of attractive cake designs available for selection, there are many decorators, as well as clients for whom the cakes are painstakingly created, who feel that as attractive as these designs are, they just don't quite fit their requirements. Others prefer that their cake is individual rather than a copy.

When a cake is required to play a part in the celebration of a special occasion, it becomes a great deal more special if it is obvious that the decorator has spent time in considering the type of occasion that is being celebrated and the personalities and interests of those involved. This personal touch allows the recipients to feel that their cake is a 'one and only' item created especially for them as well as giving the decorator a great feeling of satisfaction.

By doing this, decorators place themselves in the position of not only being expert decorators, but also designers.

Cake decorating is a highly skilled and technical art. Proficiency at such skills as applying a covering of icing, piping and moulding is essential, but, alone, will not achieve the creation of a masterpiece. Products of these skills must be carefully selected, executed and combined to produce an appealing cake. The finished cake must, as well as being an example of well executed skills, be an example of good design.

Good design does not just fall into place as work proceeds. Too often it is realised that there is something wrong only after the cake is completed—then comes the difficult task of identifying the problem and correcting it.

A decorator who produces a cake of exceptional standard is one who has mastered and perfected the required skills; who is able to recognise and understand the components or elements of design as well as demonstrate practical understanding of how to use them to best advantage; and who takes the time to plan so that the cake has appeal and displays the skills at their optimum.

The elements of design are those things which are able to be used or manipulated in order to achieve the required result. Those particularly relating to cake decoration include shape, line, colour, texture and space. Some examples are quite obvious, such as the shape of cakes and boards, lines created by ribbon, the colour of the cake cover and chosen decoration, the surface finish created by the different treatment of icings and the available area in which the decoration can be applied.

Others require closer examination in order to be recognised. A decorative fan, bells or cascading flowers are not just decorations to be applied to the top of a cake. They each form a definite shape. The fan blades and flowers create a sense of direction or line. A piped border is not just a series of stars or shells. It becomes a line. Writing or inscription is a series of lines cleverly arranged to both convey a message and contribute to the overall design.

Successful design depends on the use of these elements according to generally proven rules or principles. This does not mean that they must be applied to the letter but rather that they must be understood and the consequences of the manner in which they are applied realised.

As with most rules there are exceptions and these are perfectly acceptable if they have a purpose, achieve the desired results and the total product is still an example of good design. It must be remembered that the final product results from the application of a number of design principles to a number of elements and it is the sum of these which produces a successful cake.

Allowing that personal preferences will influence the degree of appeal which a cake will hold for any observer, the careful application of proven guidelines will result in the production of a cake that is structurally sound and aesthetically appealing within the limitations of its particular specifications.

Principles of Design

In order for any project to be successful, the materials required must be put together in the best possible way. This is achieved by applying rules which, through continued application, have proven to produce successful results.

In the field of design, these rules are known as principles. Their application to the design of cakes is no different to their application to any other project. The end product must suit the purpose for which it was created. It must be seen as a unit which is both pleasing and interesting. It must be structurally sound and visibly balanced. All parts must be in correct proportion, with each given correct emphasis so that it demands its appropriate share of attention.

This can be achieved only with a thorough understanding of the rules or principles of design and a realisation of the consequences of varied applications.

The decorator must have a clear mental picture of the desired result and then set about applying these principles in conjunction with the decorating skills required to achieve it.

A superb example of good design, this two-tiered wedding cake features lace, ribbons and floral decorations in perfect balance.

Unity

Unity in a design is the quality which gives it the power to attract and hold attention. To achieve this a feeling must be created in which all parts belong—are an integral part of the whole. Each must appear necessary and contribute in its own way to form the whole. The design must be seen in total as a single item. The observer may recognise various individual parts but still see the whole as a unit.

In order to achieve this, the various parts must be chosen so that they have characteristics in common and which form an obvious link between one part and the others and so with the whole.

Where there is more than one cake to the unit, such as a tiered wedding cake, an excellent opportunity is provided to demonstrate how unity in design works.

Although usually different in size, the cakes are generally chosen to be of the same or similar shape and the side decoration, which may reflect the feature ornament and/or floral work, is repeated on each. While there may be a specific theme ornament on the feature cake, there is usually accompanying floral decoration of similar flowers, colour and style on each component cake. These factors all contribute to building a relationship between the tiers.

Cakes of different shapes can also be used successfully if thought is given to their decoration and arrangement.

Cakes may be tiered traditionally or offset, or arranged separately at different levels but on a common base. This perpendicular assembly or the use of the common base contributes to the formation of the unit—a cake.

Unity is also seen in single celebration cakes where the colour, shape and piped side decorations are chosen to support the theme recognised in the top decoration.

Cakes of different shapes can be used successfully if thought is given to their decoration and arrangement.

Harmony and Contrast

Harmony and contrast reflect a range of combinations of a particular element from one end of the scale, where all are the same, to the other where they are totally different.

For harmony to exist there must be some relationship or agreement between the components of shape or colour or both. There should be no apparent competition for attention nor should the choice indicate merely a random selection.

Care must be taken, however, that this is not overdone. Total harmony, the use of a number of identical components, tends to become dull and uninteresting.

This may be overcome by using similar components—those which have a major common factor but are not identical.

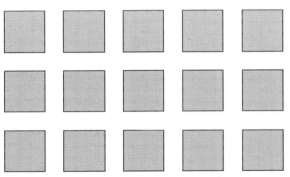

Harmony–same shapes, little interest.

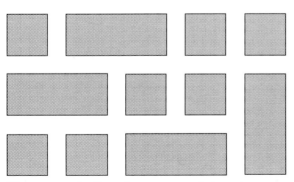

Harmony–similar shapes, more interest.

Contrast results from the use of unrelated or dissimilar components.

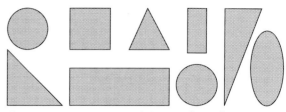

Great contrast–competition and confusion.

While a harmonious design may be quite pleasing, often a little variety will create more interest. This is done by introducing slight contrast—something that will subtly attract attention without being overpowering. The design is then given a lift—a quality of interest that will allow it to hold attention.

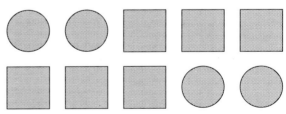

Little contrast–more interest.

However, overuse of contrast creates obvious competition between the components. This may initially attract attention but then the design becomes too much for the observer to cope with and interest is lost.

The common base or presentation board on which multiple cakes are arranged may enhance the whole picture if some relationship is evident.

The choice of a harmonious or contrasting presentation board changes the whole effect of this wedding cake.

Most tiered or multilevel cakes are examples of harmony of shape. A cake that is unrelated in shape to the others will attract attention, but unless the total design is carefully planned, that cake will stand out as being different from the rest and the appeal as a unit will be lost.

Ideally the aim is to create a design which is a complete unit, that is, mostly harmony with a small amount of contrast.

The board on which a single cake is decorated and presented is an important part of the design. Use of the wrong board shape can create an

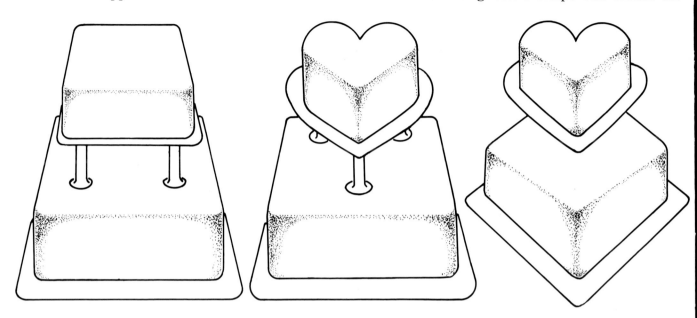

The choice of shapes and positioning of tiered cakes is important in creating harmony and interest.

The correct choice in board shape is an essential first step in creating harmony. Here we see the same cake placed on three different boards, two reflecting the shape of the cake and one in complete contrast.

uneasiness about a cake and upset the design right from the start. Choosing a board that reflects the shape of the cake is an initial step in creating harmony.

Further attention can be given to this by rounding off the harsh angles of square or other angular boards, and also by bevelling or tapering the edges of all boards so that their appearance is softer. A covered cake, unless royal icing is used, has gently rounded edges and angles. It is fitting to repeat this on the boards.

Harmony and contrast of shapes extend beyond the choice of cakes and boards. Shapes are evident in the decorative ornaments and piped decoration used and these must also be considered.

If a cake has smooth rounded edges, it is fitting to repeat this on the board.

Shapes are also evident in the top and side decorations of a cake, and so harmony in these must be considered.

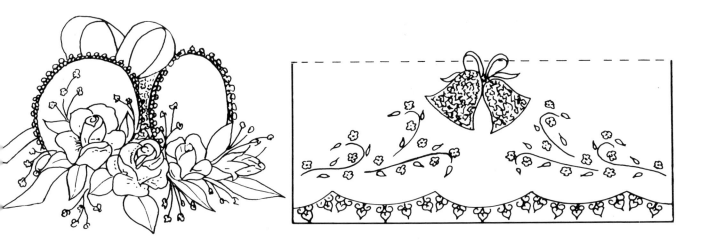

17

Similarly, the use of lines or the direction indicated by lines of piping, ribbon, etc., and the use of textures and colour must be carefully considered. Too many horizontal lines created by the decoration may create a pleasant but uninteresting cake.

Diagonals can add life to a series of horizontal lines. Overuse of diagonals may result in a feeling of discomfort because they suggest too much activity.

Designs using severe, straight lines can be softened and made to look more attractive by the use of contrasting curves.

Piped decoration and the use of stippled effects provide a raised and contrasting texture to the smooth surface of the cake cover. The use of tulle, the varying surfaces of moulded decorations and careful selection of the board covering can provide interest in this way.

Colour is an extremely important element in design as it is often responsible for initial approval or disapproval from the observer. It has enormous use, in varying combinations and strengths, to provide just enough harmony and interest to suit the situation.

It can be seen then that all parts of the design are important—the whole is dependent on each component for its success and all must contribute to a careful balance of harmony and contrast.

Designs using severe straight lines can be softened and made to appear more attractive by the use of contrasting curves.

Diagonals can add life to a series of horizontal lines.

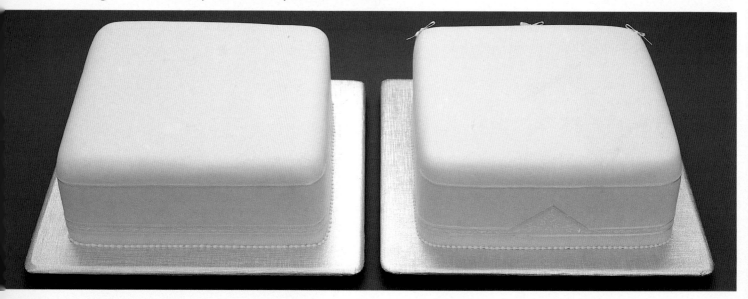

Balance

Balance refers to visual weight distribution so that the overall effect is one of stability. Each of the components of a design carries weight and so must be carefully arranged so that this stability is maintained.

Balance may be symmetrical or asymmetrical.

Symmetrical or Formal Balance

This is achieved when one half of the design is a mirror image or the exact reverse of the other. This type of balance is relatively easy to achieve and creates no feeling of discomfort as it is quickly recognised that the weight distribution within the two halves is equal. The effect of this type of balance is restful.

Symmetrical balance has a tendency to place emphasis on the centre, creating an obvious position for the desired focal point such as theme decoration or floral display.

Another effect of symmetrical balance is to appear to reduce the actual size of the design by the division into two equal parts.

This cake is an example of symmetrical balance with an imaginary central vertical line making each half a mirror image of the other.

Radial Balance

Radial balance is related to symmetrical balance in that the focus is concentrated on the centre. However, where the division which produces the identical halves in symmetrical balance is limited to the one position, the number of divisions in radial balance is limited only by the number of times the component parts are repeated around the centre.

A characteristic of radial balance is the feeling of circular movement around, towards or outwards from the focal point.

Significant use of radial balance is made in the decoration of gateaus and tortes where it is important that the removal of a wedge of the cake doesn't destroy the overall design. This is achieved because each component is a design within itself and doesn't depend upon the whole for its success. The total cake decoration is the repetition of a unit or units around the centre.

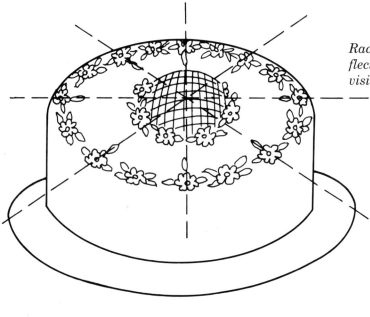

Radial balance, another example of symmetry, is reflected here, with the cake having several possible divisions through the centre.

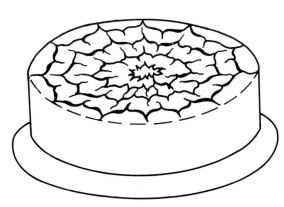

A feathering effect gives a cake circular motion.

Radial balance is also achieved where each division is identical and complete within itself.

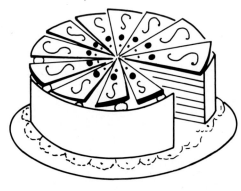

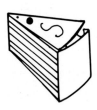

Asymmetrical or Informal Balance

When this type of balance is used, the principle of the lever of a seesaw is applied. Heavy weights near the centre are counterbalanced by lighter weights placed further away.

Asymmetrical balance is more interesting than symmetrical balance because it is not so obvious, and unconscious curiosity is aroused to see just how the balance is achieved. Movement is suggested and more freedom and flexibility in the arrangements of the parts are allowed. The result may also be more spacious or less cluttered than in a symmetrical design.

Both these cakes have the heavier top decorations counterbalanced by a smaller decoration or inscription.

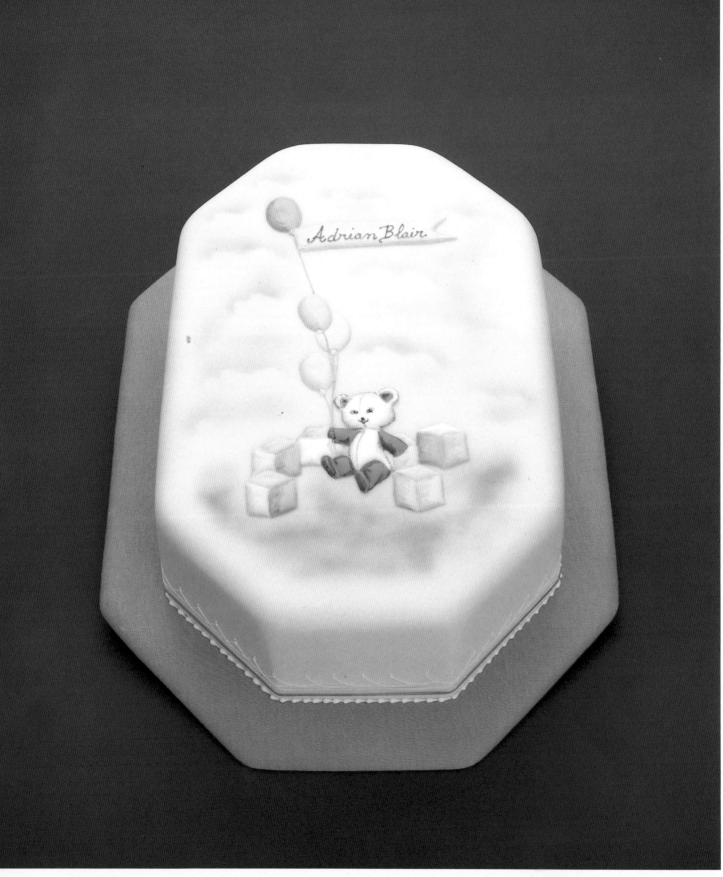

Rather than concentrate only on the top of the cake, consideration must be given to balance this weight with side decoration which seats the cake on the board.

*In this example, the airbrushed shading has been continued down the side to balance
the top design.*

There is a tendency to concentrate on the top of the cake when applying the principle of balance. While this is important, the whole cake must give the impression of stability. It must appear to be firmly seated on the base board and not give the impression of being top heavy. For this reason it is usually found that in the visual weight distribution from the side view, more weight is placed towards the base of the cake. The decoration tends to be heavier or more concentrated in this area.

When tiered or multi-level cakes are desired, not only does the design on the individual cakes need to be balanced but the overall assembled whole must form a stable unit also.

Traditionally tiered cakes are designed to form an imaginary triangle when assembled. This shape, with its wide base, is extremely stable.

When cakes are assembled in more contemporary offset styles, that is, either one cake on another or separately but on a common base, the same rule of overall balance and stability applies. It is customary, because of the obvious heavier weight of the largest cake, to use this on the bottom level. This automatically provides a feeling of stability. This is also achieved where the bottom level is actually two or more individual cakes.

Balance must also be evident within the deco-

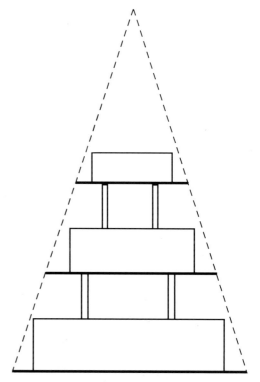

Make sure multilevel cakes form a perfect triangle. Adjust your board sizes and cake heights to achieve this.

rative ornaments placed on a cake. They must appear as a stable unit within themselves as well as contributing to the overall balance of the cake design.

These floral arrangements are examples of symmetrical and asymmetrical balance. Each side of the arrangement on the left is a mirror image while the arrangement on the right is a graduating design.

Repetition, Rhythm and Progression

Repetition

Repetition is simply the use of the same component several times in the same design. In doing this harmony is achieved and the eye recognises the similarities, and vision tends to flow from one part to the next.

Too much exact repetition tends to be dull and uninteresting. This can be relieved by alternating similar or contrasting parts.

Too little or no repetition in a design, that is using all or mostly contrasting parts, leads to confusion.

When there is repetition or alternation of components, evenly spaced, at the same angle and in the same direction, rhythm is created.

Rhythm

Rhythm is achieved when vision is encouraged to flow smoothly from one area of a design to another. It appears as organised movement and this helps to create continuity in design.

Rhythm in design is developed by using two other factors, repetition and progression.

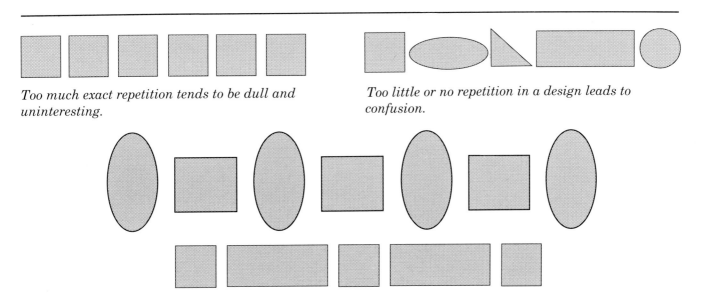

Too much exact repetition tends to be dull and uninteresting.

Too little or no repetition in a design leads to confusion.

Relieve exact repetition by alternating similar or contrasting parts.

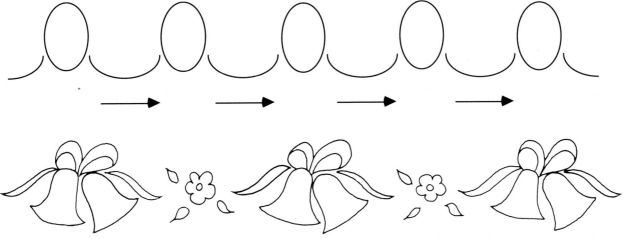

Rhythm is created when there is repetition or alternation of components evenly spaced, at the same angle and in the same direction.

Pattern

When two or more units are repeated side by side a pattern emerges. The use of an odd number of units is more interesting and has more impact than an even number. This pattern forms the basis of decorations on the sides of cakes. These repetitions may be exact, they may alternate or they may exhibit progressive changes in order to suit the particular requirement.

The same components can be arranged differently and/or graduated in size according to the requirements.

Progression

Progression suggests onwards motion towards a goal or special feature and can be used to emphasise a focal point or feature of interest.

Progression is achieved by systematically increasing or decreasing one or more of the qualities of the design. For example, size or colour of the repeated parts.

Harmony and unity result from rhythmic repetition and progression.

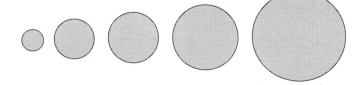

The same component shown in progressive sizes. This creates motion.

Progressive increase in flower size to focal point.

Proportion

Proportion refers to the relationship of one part of the design to the whole and to other parts of it. If the size or quantity of any part of a design does not compare favourably then the design will not be successful.

The width and height of a cake should compare favourably with each other as should the amount and thickness of the piped decoration in relation to the size of the cake.

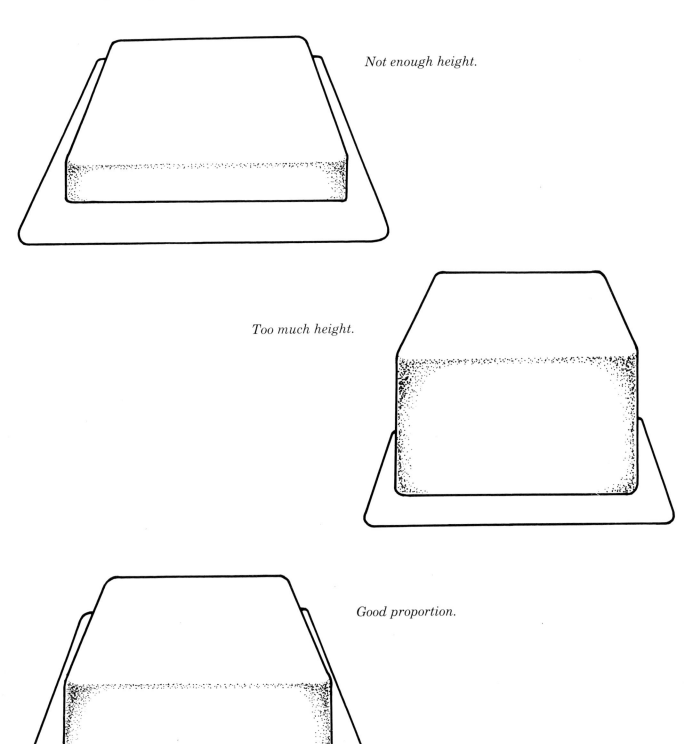

Not enough height.

Too much height.

Good proportion.

A small cake can be overwhelmed by a large, brightly coloured floral decoration while small, delicately coloured decorations or flowers may be lost on a large cake.

Proportion affects balance. A part which is too large in proportion to the rest implies extra weight—too small, not enough. The same can be said for the use of colour and concentration of any of the other elements.

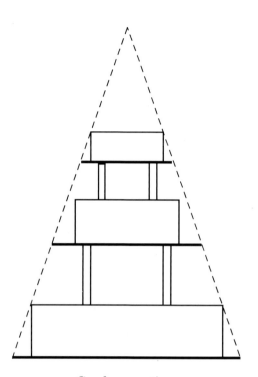

Good proportion.

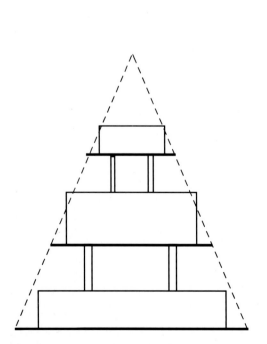

Incorrect proportion in middle cake and lower cake.

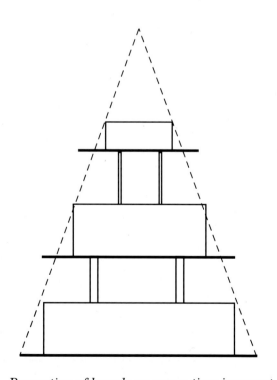

Proportion of boards on upper tiers incorrect.

A small cake can be totally overwhelmed by a large decoration. Try to proportion your designs to suit the cake size.

Emphasis

This involves deciding how important each component is to the design and then giving each a suitable degree of visual importance. More attention should be drawn to the important parts than to those of less importance.

Emphasis results in the creation of focal points and background areas and progressive degrees of interest in the areas between. Attention is attracted and held in focal areas and relaxed in others.

A simple way to make a part more obvious is to use more of it, or, to increase the value of its qualities that will attract attention.

Although both these shapes have the same colour intensity, the larger one outweighs the smaller. Also, on the right, brighter or darker colours outweigh neutral or pale colours.

A larger size will attract more attention than a smaller size and strong colours more than neutral or paler colours.

If gradual importance is given to the components in the direction of a focal area then the eye is directed towards that goal. Progressive increase in size and colour is effective in achieving this. This is particularly useful in floral sprays.

The use of symmetrical balance tends to place attention on the centre.

The focal point may be weakened, however, if the other parts of the design compete for attention by being equal to or stronger than it in qualities such as size, shape or colour.

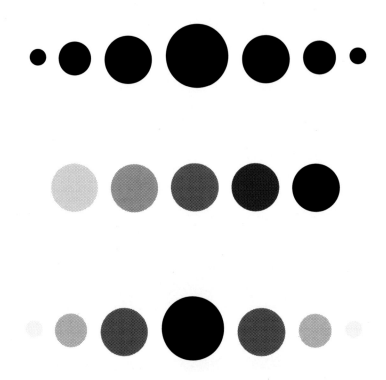

Size as well as colour can attract attention to the desired focal point.

The use of graduated sizes is useful in floral sprays.

Focal point on the left cake is weakened by other parts of design while the right cake has a strong focal point.

The focal item, the ring case, has to compete with similar-sized flowers on the left while on the right the focal item is obvious and there is no competition with the smaller flowers.

Overcrowding around the centre flower has detracted from the focal point on the left whereas on the right it has been given space to be appreciated.

Overcrowding detracts from the intended focal point, which should be obvious. The viewer should not be required to search in order to find it. Therefore it must be given space or room to be recognised and appreciated.

Background influences also play an important part. A background should support not compete with a focal area and therefore its qualities must be subdued.

Lines, real or imaginary, can direct vision to a focal point. If parts of a design are arranged so that they form lines in the required direction then they will indicate where attention is to be focused.

Care must be taken not to overuse background decoration, even if subtle as shown on the left. This can detract from the focal point unless arranged carefully.

Elements of Design

In the design of a cake it must be remembered that those items which are produced by the application of decorating skills to various sugar media, together with other accessories such as ribbons, pillars, etc., are actually examples of the elements of design.

Naturally, the decorator will feel a great sense of satisfaction in creating a beautifully moulded and coloured rose, an intricate filigree butterfly or extremely fine piped embroidery. If these are to be used effectively they must be seen in their actual role.

The colour of the rose is important. This will have considerable influence on the rest of the cake. The rose itself will not be placed as an isolated decoration. It may be featured with leaves, buds, smaller supporting flowers and ribbon to form a spray which will have a recognisable shape which can be a useful component of the overall design. The spray may also be capable of indicating an imaginary line or sense of direction so that the observer follows this from one area of the cake to another or from one tier to another.

The filigree butterfly may play an important part as a feature decoration and as such the shape can be repeated as a motif in piped embroidery or in piped lace so that the whole decoration is related.

The decorator must learn to see these products as examples of the elements of design and plan and execute them as part of the whole picture if an outstanding cake is to be the end result.

Shape

Shape refers to the identifiable and measurable outline of an object. Although there appears to be an endless variety of shapes, close examination will reveal that all show some qualities of the basic geometric shapes—the rectangle, triangle and circle.

Shapes based on a rectangle have a solid structural quality which promotes a feeling of stability and strength. These qualities also tend to reflect some harshness which may, in some cases, be undesirable.

The basic rectangular or square shape promotes a feeling of restfulness. However, if it is placed diagonally it becomes more dynamic.

Angular shapes are dramatic. They imply motion and restlessness and attract attention.

Circular or curved shapes are restful and have a gentle and smooth flowing, rhythmical quality.

Shapes can play a part in reflecting and supporting moods, personalities and theme situations. Careful thought in the choice of a cake shape can contribute enormously to the success of the design.

Remember that decorative ornaments, flowers, floral sprays and piped decorations all produce shapes and these are useful as such in creating a design.

Line

Lines have several vital functions in design. These include:

Forming Boundaries

The definition of areas is achieved by lines. We recognise a particular cake shape by the line which encloses it. A line defines the top of a cake from the side and also from the board. Without these linear boundaries we are faced with an infinite space. Once the boundaries have been defined the task of design can begin.

All decorations on a cake produce lines and shapes which must be used correctly if crowding and confusion is to be avoided. Similarly, too little use of line and shape produces a dull and uninteresting design.

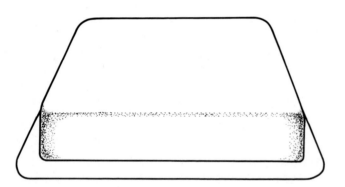 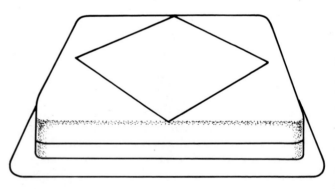

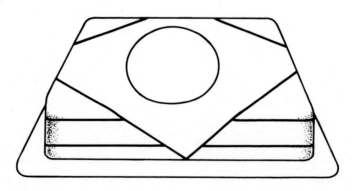

Dividing an Area into Smaller Parts of Interest

Having recognised the boundaries within which we are to work we may find that this defined area is still too large to be interesting. We then set about dividing it into smaller areas and applying decoration to them so that together they form an interesting whole. A cake which has no other decoration except an ornament on the top is not an item of interest. By adding piped lines of decoration or attaching lengths of ribbon we are forming smaller areas from the whole. The eye can then move from one area to another, viewing each individually and as part of the whole design. Thus, interest in the cake is created.

If there are too few divisions then the design lacks interest.

If there are too many, the design becomes crowded and confusing.

Creating Optical Illusions

Vertical lines create height while horizontal lines reduce height. While it is better to begin with a cake that is in correct proportion, vertical and horizontal lines can be quite useful if we are required to decorate a cake that is too low or one that is a little too high and cutting to reduce the height is unacceptable.

The shape of a cake can be altered by the use of horizontal and vertical lines. The cake on the right appears higher because the vertical lines draw attention to the sides.

Long horizontal lines and ribbons are restful and relaxing. They break the sides into smaller areas that can be viewed separately as well as part of the whole.

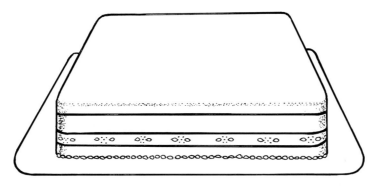

The flowing curves on each tier of this wedding cake draw the eye upwards towards the top decoration which is also slightly curved. This produces a cake of superb design.

Suggesting Motion

a. Horizontal lines tend to be restful and relaxing, particularly if the lines are long.

   A strip of ribbon attached around a cake is a simple way of achieving this effect. If a piped line of decoration is applied close to, and parallel to, the ribbon, or, if a second strip of ribbon is applied similarly, the effect will be reinforced.

b. Curves have a smooth flowing, graceful and rhythmical quality.

   Horizontal curves suggest gently relaxed movement.

   Long upward curves promote a feeling of inspiration and an uplifting quality to the design. Long downward curves tend to be more serious although comfortable in that they imply solid attachment to the base.

   Short curves suggest an air of playfulness.

Horizontal curves create a feeling of grace and rhythm. When swung upwards they lift attention to the top of the cake while downward curves link the cake to the base and can be helpful in balancing a heavy top decoration.

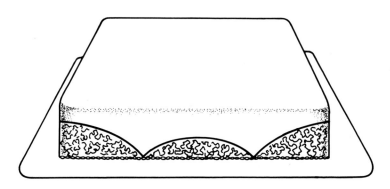

c. Vertical lines suggest strength and stability. Any line created by vertical decoration reinforces the feeling that the cake is firmly seated on the base.

d. Diagonal lines suggest movement and activity. They provide an effective contrast when used with horizontal lines and can be quite dramatic.

The vertical lines on the sides of this cake seat it firmly on the base and when combined with the diagonal lines an effective contrast is achieved.

Here we have a combination of horizontal and diagonal lines around the sides of this cake. The effect is quite dramatic.

Directing Vision

An important quality of any line is its direction. Good composition in design should direct vision to the focal point.

When the eye makes contact with a line it tends to follow it and this is useful in directing attention to the desired point. It is also useful if we wish to direct attention to, or away from, a particular area. Diagonal lines are particularly effective in doing this.

Where lines converge the vision is automatically drawn to that point and this becomes a focal point. For this to be complete there must be some feature on which to focus.

Lines or lines of sight may be actual or apparent, that is, there may be a piped line or a line of ribbon or an imaginary line created by a number of components. For example, small piped decorations placed close together in a continuous path form a line of vision.

Connecting Various Parts of a Design

Repeating a piped motif several times around the side of a cake may serve to fill the space and may be related to other parts of the decoration, but they tend to be seen as individuals rather than a unit if there is no connecting line for the eye to follow.

Just as a leaf is not part of a floral spray if there is no stem to connect it, side motifs need to be linked to one another if they are to be part of a whole. Ribbon and piped lines, real or imaginary, will do this and then the eye will follow the direction of the pattern around the cake.

While considering the important role which lines play in design we must still be conscious that harmony is important. Lines which are related or have related direction provide harmony. Those which are unrelated or have no related direction provide contrast.

Side motifs can appear to be unrelated and seen as individual if not joined by some form of connecting line. Here ribbon and piping have been used but any repetitive pattern is acceptable if it links the large items.

When a cake has many offset tiers, the floral sprays should be positioned to create a flowing line from one tier to another.

Space

Space, although rather intangible, is an important part of design. It suggests freedom of movement and room to breathe, and allows part of a design to be displayed and appreciated without being crowded and overwhelmed by others.

Common problems associated with space may appear to be an excess or a lack of it. In actual fact the true problem is more likely to be inefficient use of the available space.

The aim in design is not to include as many of the elements or decorating skills as possible, but to select a few examples and make them work together to gain the optimum effect. Often an overall piped decoration may be improved if the number of repetitions is reduced and the decorations are spread out a little more. A floral spray may be improved by reducing the number of flowers and arranging them more effectively.

The way in which space is divided will affect the overall design. Equal division appears to split a whole into two halves. Unequal division creates interest while still maintaining the whole image.

Converging ribbon lines have been used here to draw attention to the side decoration. Because this decoration is centred it draws attention to the centre top arrangement and balances the whole design.

Continuous lacework has been used to direct attention to the corner. The placement of this floral spray balances the offset top decoration.

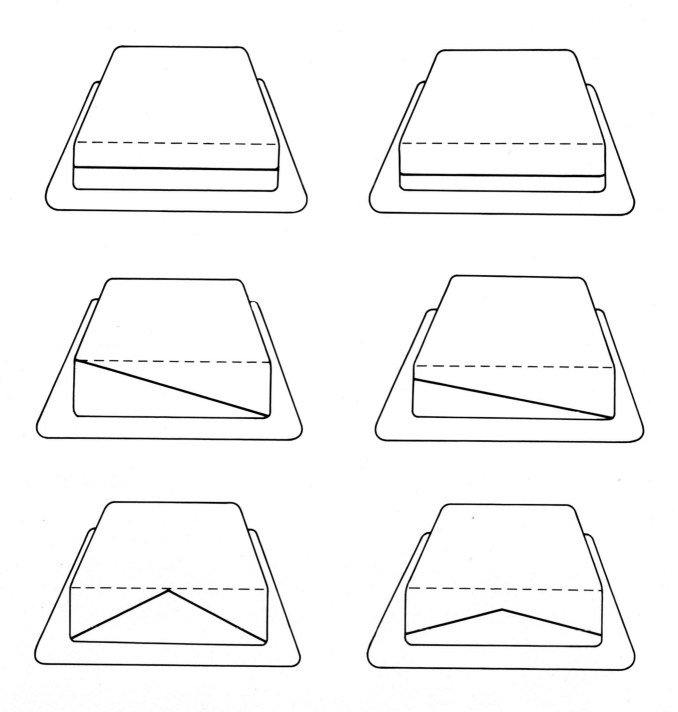

All decorations create lines and space and divide the area into shapes. When these divisions are equal the cake will be split into halves while unequal divisions create interest.

The large oval surfaces on this cake have been used perfectly by balancing the inscription against the stole on the bottom tier and the moulded card on the top.

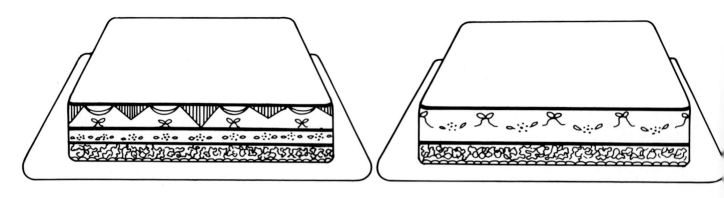

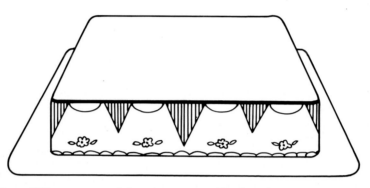

These three examples show different uses of the same space. Rather than use as many elements as possible to fill the available space it is sometimes more pleasing to the eye to select a few examples and work them together to gain a harmonious result with no overcrowding.

Texture

Every surface has a texture which has both a physical and aesthetic effect on us. Texture generally refers to how surfaces feel when they are touched but since texture results from the translation of touch, one sensory experience, into vision, another sensory experience, it can in fact be both tactile and visual.

Once textures have been experienced they tend to influence future associations.

Because of the highly fragile nature of cake decorations, recognition of textures by touching is generally discouraged so it is visual texture which plays an important role in cake design.

Effects of Texture

1. *Physical association*
   Rough surfaces may be pleasant, stimulating, harsh or irritating.

   Smooth sleek surfaces may be slippery and cold or pleasantly cooling.

   Fluffy or fuzzy surfaces may be soft and warm.

Floral sprays are usually improved by reducing the number of flowers or spreading the arrangement.

The contrast between the rough and smooth surfaces on this beautiful cake provide an interesting background for the Christmas wreath.

2. *Light reflection*

Rough surfaces absorb light to varying degrees making colours appear less bright and revealing patterns of light and dark areas.

Smooth surfaces tend to reflect light, attracting attention, causing colours to be quite clear.

3. *Imparting character and attractiveness*

Textures give surfaces a degree of individual-ity and appeal. Texture may be contributed automatically by the particular medium used, for example the smooth shiny surface of piping gel and the smooth surface of rolled plastic icing. It also may be created by making impressions into the smooth surface, by pulling the surface of a soft icing up to a point in a regular pattern or the use of a comb as on the side of a gateau.

Colour

In order to understand how colour can be used effectively in design a knowledge of colour and its qualities is necessary. The study of colour usually begins with the colour wheel.

What appears to be colourless light contains all the hues or colours of the spectrum—violet, blue, green, yellow, orange and red. These are naturally blended and balanced so that the resultant light is colourless. When this light is passed through a prism it forms separate bands of each of these colours. If these are taken and represented in order in a circle and intermediate colours are placed between them then the result is a colour wheel.

The twelve colours represented on the colour wheel are classified as primary, secondary and intermediate colours.

Primary colours are red, blue and yellow. These cannot be produced by the mixing of other colours. However, other colours can be made by mixing primary colours.

Secondary colours are made by mixing equal quantities of each of two primary colours. A mixture of red and blue gives violet, blue and yellow produce green, and yellow and red produce orange.

On the colour wheel these are placed midway between the two primary colours from which they are made.

Intermediate colours are found between the primary and secondary colours from which they are mixed. For example, blue green is made by mixing the primary colour blue with the secondary green.

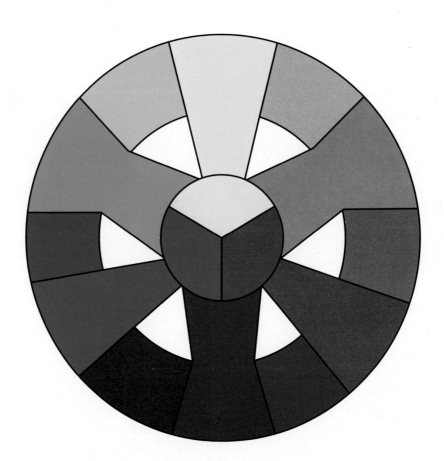

Colour wheel showing primary, secondary and intermediate colours.

New colours are produced by combining neighbouring colours. For example, blue green mentioned above can be mixed with more green or blue as desired. The range of colours available for use is therefore not limited to those illustrated on a colour wheel.

If the three primary colours are combined, or any colour is mixed with its opposite on the colour wheel, a greyed colour results.

When used in combination, colours create a range of effects from pleasant harmony to decided contrast.

If only one colour is used there is an obvious unity and harmony. This is the case with *monochromatic* colour schemes.

Two examples of monochromatic colour schemes.

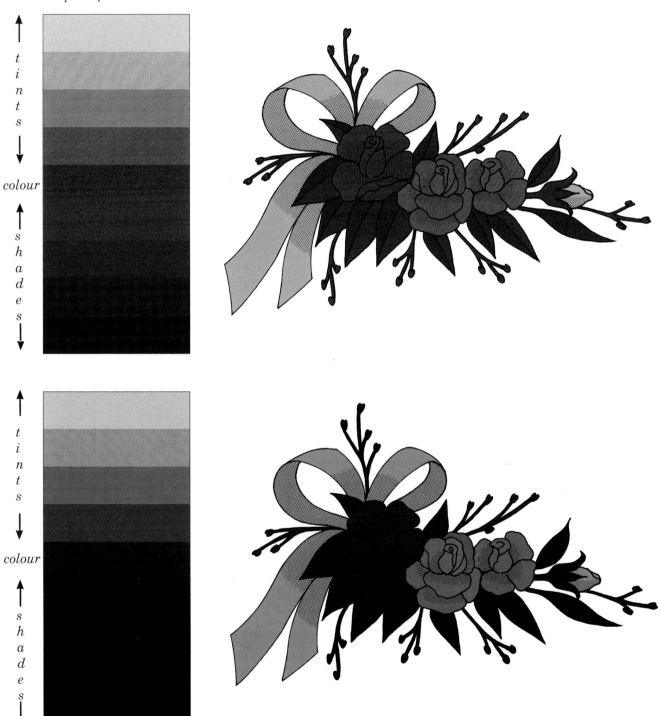

If related colours are used, that is those which lie next to or adjacent to each other on the colour wheel (e.g. red, red orange and orange) then harmony is also produced, since the colours have a common characteristic—in this case all contain red. A sequence of colour is used and such a colour scheme is referred to as *analogous*.

Analogous

Analogous

The combining of colours which lie directly opposite on the colour wheel produces contrast. The result may vary from lively interest if the area treated by each colour is small, to vivid and intense contrast if the colours cover a large area.

A colour scheme consisting of opposite colours is referred to as *complementary*.

Contrasts in colour and its qualities are useful in emphasising and defining important features.

Complementary

Complementary

Subtle use of analogous colour has produced this delightful child's cake. The extension work around the base has been topped with lace and together these two features balance the adornments on the top of the cake.

A striking example of the use of analogous colour. The converging of the ribbons and the graduation of the name add to the effect.

An airbrushed frill around the base of this key cake has been used to position the cake firmly on the base. The same colour scheme has been used on the floral spray and heart, producing a superb example of the monochromatic colour scheme.

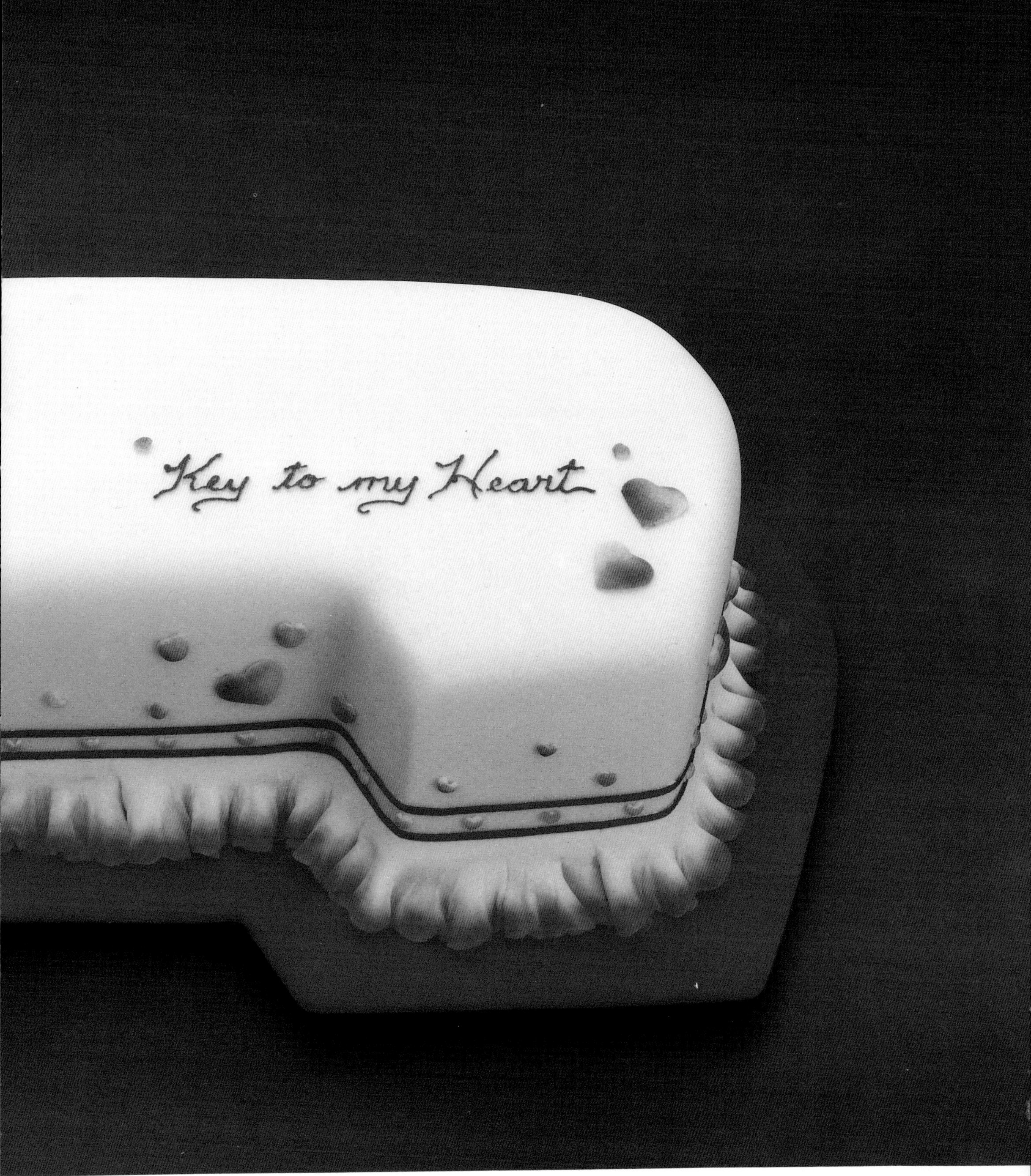
Key to my Heart

Tone or Value

The tone or value of a colour refers to the degree of lightness or darkness it exhibits, that is, its ability to reflect more or less light.

This is extremely important in a monochromatic colour scheme, which is based on one colour as the name suggests but is used so that there is a graduation of tone.

To make a colour lighter or give it a lighter tone, white is added in varying amounts. The result is called a *tint* of that colour. For example, pink is a tint of the colour red.

To make a colour darker or give it a darker tone, black is added in varying amounts. The result is called a *shade* of that colour. For example, maroon is a shade of the colour red.

A monochromatic colour scheme, therefore, is one in which a colour and tints and shades of that colour are used. While there is harmony because the same colour is used over and over again, there is contrast provided by the tonal variation.

Some colours are naturally darker or have more value than others. For example, yellow has the lightest tone or value on the colour wheel, violet has the darkest.

Colour values are affected by the background on which they are presented, that is, the pale pink of a rose would appear much darker on a white cake than on dark red velvet.

A monochromatic colour scheme used for a golden celebration. A diagonal sweep of ribbon and lace across the front of this bell-shaped cake draws attention to the inscription. The positioning of the floral spray on the opposite corner balances the design.

Intensity

The intensity of a colour refers to the degree to which it differs from grey, that is, its purity or strength. For example, sky blue can be vivid or strong or it can be greyed or neutralised.

The full intensity of a colour is only possible at the normal tone or value of the colour with no addition of white or black. It may then be described as being strong or high. All colours on the colour wheel are shown at their fullest intensity.

The more a colour is neutralised or greyed the lower or weaker the intensity becomes.

Intensity may be decreased by the addition of white, grey or black (tints and shades have less intensity than the colour from which they are produced) or by adding varying amounts of the complementary colour.

Intensity may be increased by adding more of the dominant colour or may appear increased if the object is placed in contrast with its complementary colour, a neutral colour or a greyed tone of the colour.

Colours promote sensations or temperature and other associated feelings. Those containing red seem warm while those containing blue seem cool.

There is a feeling of closeness with warm colours. The effect created when large areas are treated with strong warm colours is one of reduced size of advancement or closeness. Small items of strong warm colours appear to increase in size and become more dominant.

With the use of cool colours there is a feeling of distance, of recession. Large areas treated with pale cool colours tend to appear larger and more distant. Small items appear smaller and less significant.

Warm colours make the edges of items seem less sharp or defined than cool colours.

Colours are also considered to have an affinity with particular seasons:

Spring — colours of new growth and life—yellow, pale green, lilac.

Summer — bright gay colours which suggest warmth, fun and activity—pink, yellow, orange, red and dark green.

Autumn — those which suggest a slowing down of activity. Autumn suggests falling leaves and associated colours—yellow, gold and brown.

Winter — coolness—white, pale blues and greens. Sharp contrast as suggested by snow—white, red, blue and green.

Choosing Colours

The use of colour can be extremely exciting and rewarding but it must be remembered that although decorated cakes may be artistic masterpieces they are also items of food. When related to food the use of colour must be in moderation.

The senses must be able to make the transition from visual attractiveness to anticipated taste attractiveness. The use of extreme colour combinations and too much strong colour may adversely influence this.

Colour is a major factor in the successful design and decoration of cakes. Even if all other aspects of the design are perfect, indiscriminate use of colour can destroy the whole appeal. Through colour certain features can be emphasised or played down, appearances altered and aesthetic influences gained.

Attention can be attracted or directed to important features on a cake by the use of clear, bright or intense colours as well as those that are dark. Warm colours reinforce this because of the advancing and stimulating qualities.

For background areas the reverse is generally desirable, so colours with less forceful, restful and receding qualities are used. Appropriate use of colour in a floral spray will not only draw attention to the whole spray as a feature but will also contribute to the focal area. Even if the feature decoration is not floral, the use of colour functions in the same way.

In order that the colours used to attract attention can work efficiently, the background or overall covering colour of the cake must be chosen so that it contributes to and does not compete with the decoration. The use of pale colours or, more correctly, tints, and those colours which are less intense will do this. White is a popular choice for a cake cover as it provides no competition for the colours used in the decoration. The board or base on which the cake is presented forms part of the background or support area and it must contribute to the overall scheme.

Striking contrasts also attract attention and can be very dramatic. Contrasts can be made between a background and the feature to be emphasised. They can also exist within the featured decoration which can be displayed effectively on a background which is neutral, related to one of the contrasting colours or related to both. For example, blue and orange create a striking contrast on a pale 'tint of brown' background.

In altering appearances, the qualities of advancing and receding and the effect of different intensities and values of colour are useful.

In its aesthetic effect the appeal of colour to the senses is used, for example, warmth, cool-ness, softness and harshness. This can be reinforced by teaming colour with appropriate textures.

Colour can also be used to give weight to certain areas and contribute to balance. Dark colours or those with darker tone or value carry more weight than light colours, and colours of high intensity carry more weight than those of low intensity.

In symmetrical balance, the centre or focal area is generally weighted more heavily with colour as well as by its obvious size or apparent physical weight. Where decorations are asymmetrically balanced, the use of colour must also be balanced.

The use of coloured ribbon, piped decoration or frills towards the base of a cake also adds to the weight and stability of the cake.

A simple birthday cake for Grandma in a complementary colour scheme. The extension work and lace offset the pansy and handkerchief on top. The addition of fine satin ribbon completes the effect.

Masterpiece of Design

There are many reasons for decorating cakes—pure self-satisfaction in the work done, pleasure gained in delighting the recipient, a means of earning extra income or for competition purposes.

Whatever the reason, the decorator soon realises that the task is not merely the decoration of a cake but also its design. Even if a cake style is copied, it is usually found that there will be differences, either by choice or because the particular cake does not lend itself exactly to that style.

It is estimated that in allocating points for effort and ability in the production of a successfully designed and decorated cake, approximately half is given to the level of skill in practical execution of the various techniques and the remainder to the selection and putting together of the products of this skill.

An example of technical expertise and excellent design skills, this two-tiered wedding cake has been made in a cushion shape. The lace work around the edges continues the downward slope of the cushion and both tiers have been tilted forward. The single deep red rose on the top overhangs the bottom tier with ribbon, completing this masterpiece of design.

Impact

The first test of this expertise in selecting and putting the whole together is in the first impression gained by the viewer, or the impact. This is a fairly dramatic word but it fits the situation well.

Without looking too closely into detail an opinion is formed—the cake may be liked or disliked to varying degrees or it may create no definite impression at all. There may be uncertainty but curiosity is aroused so that a closer look is called for.

If the cake is for competition purposes, the impact must be great and favourable. There must be something about the cake that makes it special, that sets it apart from the rest. A great deal of time must be spent in planning. The decorator must know exactly what is required in the finished masterpiece and then set about achieving that goal.

Impact is influenced by:

Presentation

Once the first impression has been gained, examination then begins in search of support of this.

The cake presentation usually then comes under scrutiny. Presentation covers many facets—

- Does the cake reflect neatness, polish and appropriate thought and care in its creation?

- Is it situated so that it may be fully appreciated?

- Is the base on which it is presented appropriate in size, shape, colour and surface?

- Is it structurally sound—is it level? If tiered, does it appear balanced and stable?

- Is there suitable use of colour?

- Are all aspects in proportion?

- Is the correct amount of emphasis placed on each part?

- Is the overall picture one of interest and harmony and suited to the theme?

In other words, is the cake of good design? Has the decorator taken the time to recognise, understand and then apply the relevant concepts?

Individuality and Creativity

These reflect the decorator's efforts in extending creative and technical ability.

The result may be:

a. *Something new*. Here the decorator shows ability to experiment and create. New ideas and techniques are always in demand and credit will be awarded.

b. *Something different*. This may be something new, a whole new concept or it may be an idea or technique that is already used but presented in a new way. Here the decorator is saying, 'I am not a copybook artist. I can do that too and do it well. Mine is better and more interesting and appealing.'
   This is also extremely creditable.

c. *Something classic*. There are many well-worn design ideas and techniques that are always popular and acceptable, and present a pleasing picture. However, if a decorator is not aiming to prove initiative and worth as a designer as well as a technician then absolute perfection in practical skills must be the goal.

If a cake has scored favourably so far, it is well on the way to being successful. What remains is the execution of practical skills.

Technical Expertise

There are no short cuts for developing practical skills. Sound instruction, determination and practice are the requirements. As well as for perfection in executing these skills, credit will always be awarded for mastering more difficult, and new applications of, techniques.

It must be remembered that the techniques involved in the decoration of cakes are skills. The optimum development and maintenance of these skills takes time and regular and continued practice. It may involve periods of frustration when things just don't work properly or which may be due to outside and uncontrollable influences such as marked and undesirable weather changes or just that a rest and a fresh start is in order. In spite of this, the dedication required in the development of these skills produces extremely enjoyable and rewarding results—both for the decorator and the recipient of the work.

To produce a truly satisfactory result cake design and decoration must be enjoyed. It will not be achieved in periods of waning interest and frustration. Such times demand a break rather than having the task become a chore.

A true masterpiece really glows with the care and attention which has been lavished on it and the enjoyment and satisfaction which its creator has achieved in its execution and completion.